Contents

A global view

In many ways, countries behave like companies or even families. Some become successful or rich, while others find it harder to achieve their goals. They need to earn and spend money to look after themselves, and often borrow money to make ends meet – or to help put their plans into practice.

The parallels can go further. Just as some families help cousins or other relatives who are needy, countries often find ways to help those less well off than themselves. This help can come in many forms, but the two most common routes are through aid and international loans.

Developing links

Why do countries send money to others, especially when poor people live within their own borders? The answer is complicated, and some people object to their taxes being spent in that way. Experts cite two main reasons for helping other countries.

One reason is related to fairness. Many people find it hard to live in a world where the people of some countries seem to be condemned to live with sickness and in poverty. Another motive for helping other countries is linked to self-interest, but it is no less effective for that. The richest nations – especially those in western Europe and North America – are often called developed countries because they developed their industries earliest and those developed industries have provided wealth for centuries. Many of the poorest countries, by contrast, are called developing countries because they are in the process of developing new ways of building their economies.

Many developed countries are happy to give developing countries a boost because the extra money will speed up the process of development.

WORLD ECONOMY EXPLAINED

International Aid and Loans

Sean Connolly

FRANKLIN WATTS
LONDON·SYDNEY

 An Appleseed Editions book

First published in 2010 by Franklin Watts
338 Euston Road, London NW1 3BH

Franklin Watts Australia
Hachette Children's Books
Level 17/207 Kent St, Sydney, NSW 2000

Created by Appleseed Editions Ltd,
Well House, Friars Hill, Guestling,
East Sussex TN35 4ET

Designed by Helen James
Edited by Mary-Jane Wilkins
Picture research by Su Alexander

ISBN 978 1 4451 0044 9

Dewey Classification: 338.9'1

A CIP catalogue for this book is available from the British Library.

Photograph acknowledgements
page 7 James Leynse/Corbis; 8 & 11 Bettmann/Corbis; 12 Peter Dench for
Football's Hidden Story/Corbis; 14 Gavid Hellier/Robert Harding World Imagery/
Corbis; 16 Jason Lee/Reuters/Corbis; 19 Steve Raymer/Corbis; 20 Getty Images;
23 Reuters/Corbis; 24 Eye Ubiquitous/Alamy; 27 AFP/Getty Images; 29 Howard
Burditt/Reuters/Corbis; 30 Reuters/Corbis; 32 Eric Draper/White House/Handout/
CNP/Corbis; 35 Justin Lane/epa/Corbis; 37 Mark Peterson/Corbis; 38 Will & Deni
McIntyre/Corbis; 41 Gideon Mendel/Corbis; 42 AFP/Getty Images
Front cover Ali Ali/epa/Corbis

Printed in China

Franklin Watts is a division of Hachette Children's Books,
an Hachette UK company.
www.hachette.co.uk

One result of greater wealth in developing countries is more people who can afford to buy the goods produced in the developed countries.

What's in a name?

The aid that flows from richer to poorer countries can follow several different paths – either from one government to another, or from a richer country to an international organization and then on to a poorer country. It might not even go through governments – some aid is donated by people directly to organizations who then distribute it to specific projects in developing countries. Whatever the origins of the money, it is usually called development aid, to distinguish it from humanitarian aid, which is raised and distributed in response to a specific crisis such as an earthquake or hurricane.

Development aid and loans aim to go to the causes of problems and help the poorest people in the world find ways of breaking out of their cycle of poverty and ill health. As people around the world – both rich and poor – struggle through difficult times, it is important to see whether this aid has succeeded in its aims, and whether we can afford to continue it.

Shoppers in developed countries often overlook the fact that billions of people will never see the range of goods on display in supermarkets like this one in a suburb of New York City.

Helping others

The idea of helping those less fortunate than ourselves is thousands of years old, and it lies at the heart of many of the world's great religions. Perhaps because of this ancient tradition, many people believe that richer countries have helped poorer countries for centuries. That view is mistaken – international aid is a relatively new idea. It started at the end of the Second World War and has developed since then.

Opposite: German families wait for a US Air Force plane to land in West Berlin in late 1948. Two and a half million West Berliners relied on supply planes while their city was blockaded by East Germany's communist government.

The international age

The horrors of the Second World War, in which more than 70 million people died around the world, made people look for ways to promote peace – or at least to avoid terrible conflicts – in the future. In 1945, even before the last shot had been fired in that war, representatives of 50 countries organized the launch of the United Nations, or UN. Since those first meetings in San Francisco, the United Nations has grown to include 192 member states.

As part of its aim to promote peace and development, the UN uses some of the money it collected from its member states to help its neediest members. The amount a country contributes depends on its size and wealth. UN organizations focus on specific areas such as farming, trade, health and children to try to ensure that the countries and regions most in need receive this aid.

A year before international representatives put the finishing touches to the new UN charter in San Francisco, another conference was held across the United States – in Bretton Woods, New Hampshire. The representatives at Bretton Woods set up the World Bank and the International Monetary Fund (IMF). These two international organizations work with large amounts of money – like the UN, members contribute money. Both the World Bank and IMF can lend money to member states when they run into trouble. Any member state can borrow from the IMF, but the World Bank only lends to developing countries. These loans help needy countries to plan their long-term development, although both organizations often set strict conditions before they release the money (see pages 16-19).

National efforts

The United States also launched a massive aid programme after the Second World War. The US had suffered much less than other powerful countries during the war, and it set up a fund to help

European countries rebuild their economies. This fund was officially called the European Recovery Program, but it came to be known as the Marshall Plan, after the US government official, George Marshall, who developed it.

Beginning in 1947, the United States distributed $13 billion among 18 European countries. In theory, this money was meant to be loaned and eventually paid back (though on generous terms). In reality, most of the money was never paid back and it came to be considered as aid. The US had several motives for setting up the project. One was a sincere wish to see European nations recover. Second was a more selfish aim – if Europeans became more prosperous, they could buy more American goods. Finally, the late 1940s were the beginning of the cold war. The Americans wanted to strengthen European nations so that they would not be tempted to elect communist governments. The Soviet Union was also offered Marshall Plan aid, but it began sending its own aid to other countries.

Money as a weapon

International aid was often linked to the rivalries and tensions of the cold war, which meant that it often became political. For example, the US or one of its allies might offer aid or loans to a Middle Eastern country – so long as the country receiving the aid allowed western oil companies to operate there. The aid was sometimes even more closely connected to the intense military rivalry between the US and the Soviet Union. To receive aid from the west or from communist sources, African, Asian or south American countries often had to agree to allow military bases or weapons within their borders.

Opposite: US Secretary of State George Marshall receives his honorary degree at Harvard University in June 1947. In his speech at Harvard, he mapped out a US foreign aid policy that became known as the Marshall Plan.

Personal account

PROTECTING FREEDOM

George Marshall, the US Secretary of State who developed what became known as the Marshall Plan, addressed the graduating students of Harvard University on 5 June 1947.

His words go further than simply defining the aims of the plan; they stand as a powerful defence of international aid at any time: 'It is logical that the United States should do whatever it is able to do to assist in the return of normal economic health in the world, without which there can be no political stability and no assured peace. Our policy is directed not against any country or doctrine but against hunger, poverty, desperation, and chaos. Its purpose should be the revival of a working economy in the world so as to permit the emergence of political and social conditions in which free institutions can exist.'

From nation to nation

Most international aid and loans fall
into one of two main categories: bilateral aid or multilateral aid. The prefix *bi* in the word bilateral means two, so bilateral aid means a relationship between two countries, with money or services going from one to another. Multilateral aid refers to money flowing from an international organization (such as the United Nations or World Bank) to one or more countries. The cost of such aid is shared by members of the organization.

Personal account

CONSTANT PRESSURE

When the Labour party won the UK general election in 1997, it promised to increase Britain's foreign aid budget. Twelve years later, it proudly announced that Britain's foreign aid budget had doubled and that the government had many more ambitious projects. Part of the reason for Britain's progress during those first 12 years was the result of pressure from aid activists.

One campaigner for increased aid was Bob Geldof, who organized the Live Aid event in 1985 (see pages 20-23). Over the years, he has continued to push governments and ordinary people to do more to help the poorest countries, especially in Africa. In 2004, he spoke about the British government's new Commission for Africa, which was set up to look at the role of foreign aid in that continent. He set that aim against Britain's existing foreign aid contribution.

'If you really want to get rid of the scars and you want the Commission for Africa to have credibility, if you want to get to next year without me and the activists and the churches screaming at you about this lot, then the minimum you do is you take the fourth richest country in the world and you measure it against its pathetic ranking as the eleventh most generous. All this appears incredibly simple and it is as simple as that.'

Opposite: Indonesian schoolchildren sit in their new schoolhouse in Banda Aceh. The school was built with foreign aid funds after the previous school was destroyed in the tsunami of 2004.

The amount of money that flows into the neediest nations can be hard to track. It changes from year to year and can be difficult to monitor. For example, humanitarian aid – immediate responses to emergencies – is not counted as part of the total. Development aid, by contrast, is intended for longer-term projects such as increasing literacy, helping farmers grow more crops or building new industries in poorer countries. Some countries include military aid (such as weapons and military vehicles) in their aid figures, but most do not.

Despite the grey areas, we can draw some conclusions. One is that bilateral aid makes up about 70 per cent of all development aid, while multilateral aid accounts for most of the other 30 per cent. Developing countres receive between £70 and £90 billion of bilateral aid every year, and between £25 and £30 billion in multilateral aid.

Norwegians gather in the capital, Oslo, to celebrate their National Day (17 May). It is a source of national pride that Norway is one of the most generous aid donors in the world.

Goals to aim for

Although countries give more in bilateral than in multilateral aid, international organizations still have an effect on the amount that countries devote to aid. The UN has set developed countries a target: each should aim to spend 0.7 per cent of their wealth (measured in gross domestic product or GDP) on overseas aid every year.

YOUR MONEY'S WORTH

How much is it worth?

The UN goal is that 0.7 per cent of every developed country's GDP should be spent on overseas aid every year. Do you think this is a reasonable figure? Is it too high, especially during difficult economic times?

Another international group, called the Organization for Economic Cooperation and Development (OECD), looks at the amount and type of aid that richer countries give to developing countries. The OECD calls this aid official development assistance and it tracks how close countries come to achieving the UN target of 0.7 per cent of GDP.

Like many statistics, the numbers sometimes appear to give conflicting evidence. The latest OECD figures for donor aid are for 2008. There are few surprises in the list of largest aid donors: they are the US, Germany, the UK, France and Japan. But only five countries – Denmark, Luxembourg, the Netherlands, Norway and Sweden – gave 0.7 per cent of their GDP. If the countries in the first list contributed in the same proportion as those in the second list, the developing world would receive billions of pounds more every year.

Opposing voices

Bilateral aid can be limited when the people who oppose aid have a greater effect on a national government than international organizations do. Not all developing countries have a say in aid amounts. Some critics of aid argue that this is not an effective way of helping a country to improve. Others argue that aid often props up inefficient governments or brutal dictators. Donor countries sometimes impose conditions on their aid as a way of avoiding these problems (for example, guarantees that money will be spent on deserving projects), but critics argue these conditions are not enough.

Agreeing terms

An old saying goes: 'there's no such thing as a free lunch.' This means that in every deal or transaction, even when something seems to be given away, there is a price to pay. The saying holds true in the world of international aid.

Some rich individuals may decide to give their money away on a whim, but national governments and international organizations have to justify what they do to voters or to member states. They want their aid – whether it is a grant or a loan to be repaid – to be effective.

和国卫生部
th, P.R.China

比尔及梅琳达·盖茨基
Bill & Melinda Gates Found

中国·北京
Beijing.China
2009.04.01

Mr.Bill Gates

One of the first steps in giving aid takes place months, if not years, before any money changes hands. The governments of developing countries discuss their needs with representatives of donor countries or international organizations such as the United Nations or World Bank. Together they focus on both needs and strategies to help development in the future. Occasionally two or more developing countries form a group to make a case for aid in each nation. These groupings can be geographical (involving countries from South America or southern Africa, for example) or they might stress some historical links. Commonwealth countries have a shared background within the British Empire; African, Caribbean and Pacific (ACP) countries formerly had ties with European countries.

Opposite: Bill Gates (right) and Chen Zhu, the Chinese Minister of Health, announce the signing of a partnership between the Bill and Melinda Gates Foundation and the Chinese government on 1 April 2009. The aim is to combat and treat tuberculosis in China.

Once they have identified problem areas and long-term solutions, developing countries and the countries who are going to help them then decide on specific projects or programmes. These might range from providing mosquito nets in a region (to combat malaria) to training teachers and buying mobile classrooms (to boost education in rural areas). The cost of these projects is added up, and then the nature of the aid (outright grant or long-term loan) is agreed.

Conditions, conditions

Most people have received money, presents or privileges which were subject to certain restrictions, or conditions. It might be as simple as 'you can have that ice cream as long as you finish your vegetables' or it might involve a deal set out over a longer period. Some parents, for example, offer to give their children a sum of money on their twenty-first birthday on condition that they do not start smoking.

Similarly, governments and international organizations often lay down conditions when they give or lend money to developing countries.

Sharpening the focus

In 1974, the south Asian nation of Bangladesh endured a terrible famine, during which as many as 1.5 million people died. International aid, which is often accompanied by complicated terms and conditions, would not have reached the worst-affected people in time to help them. So the Food and Agriculture Organization (FAO – a branch of the United Nations) organized the World Food Conference.

Most countries sent representatives to the gathering, which had two main aims – organizing a fast response to the Bangladeshi famine and finding ways to focus on global hunger. Three years later, the UN established the International Fund for Agricultural Development (IFAD) as a specialized agency. Its objective was to establish a fund 'to finance agricultural development projects primarily for food production in developing countries'.

The IFAD, based in Rome, has a specific aim: to combat poverty and hunger by helping the rural poor in the poorest regions of the world. Along with the IMF, World Bank and other multilateral lending institutions, it has pledged to reduce the proportion of the extremely poor people in the world by half by 2015.

Many of these conditions are based on common sense: for example, making sure that some of the aid is used to fight corruption in developing countries. In the past, huge amounts of aid money were wasted on bribes and inefficient government departments (which might order some essential goods twice and forget to order others). Making sure that funds go more directly to the people and projects that need them is essential, and it has become a common condition of modern aid packages.

Wider-ranging conditions, however, can range from the realm of common sense into the world of politics. Critics of the IMF claim that some of the tough conditions it has imposed on developing

countries amount to unacceptable political interference. The IMF, World Bank and other international organizations often take on the political views of their most powerful members.

During the 1980s, for example, Conservative politicians governed the UK, US and several other powerful countries. These countries had enormous influence on IMF and World Bank decisions. It became common for IMF conditions to push developing countries to adopt similar political policies, such as imposing spending cuts or privatizing industries.

A mother and her child wait outside a Red Cross food distribution point in Bangladesh during the famine of 1974. The famine led to the founding of the International Fund for Agricultural Development (IFAD).

People to people

The dull financial terms which define international aid can sometimes make the whole process seem like a business deal. They do little to conjure up images of children being taught in a purpose-built school, or of farms finally providing good harvests, or of villagers being able to sell their goods to the outside world for the first time. What's missing is the human element, although the whole point of international aid is to improve people's living conditions.

Many people who have nothing to do with governments or international organizations are eager to help others in the developing world. Some, especially young people, even travel to far-off countries to work in field hospitals, rural schools or on farming projects. Others can't give their time, but can contribute money. Their intention is the same: to reach out to others and to help make the future brighter for some of the poorest people in the world.

Looking back – and forward

The willingness to give money to help others goes back to the charitable roots of international aid – back to a time when giving had more to do with churches and less to do with national governments. Some of the earliest attempts to send money from Europe and North America to poorer countries had a religious aim – to convert people in the developing world. Nowadays, people's voluntary donations have much more to do with their sense of fairness and justice.

Opposite: Carl Hayman (back left) and Doug Howlett of the All Blacks (the New Zealand national rugby side) join in a friendly game with South African schoolchildren as part of a Save the Children school project.

YOUR MONEY'S WORTH

Letting governments off the hook?

Some people argue that private charities should not need to become involved with international aid. They believe that such groups end up doing the job which should be done by national governments and international organizations such as the United Nations.

In their view, the involvement of voluntary private charities allows national and international organizations to be less generous with their money because voluntary, private efforts will do the rest. Do you agree with this view, or do you think that they provide a necessary – and extra – level of help?

Live Aid and beyond

In late 1984, pop singers Bob Geldof and Midge Ure watched a distressing news bulletin about a famine in the East African nation of Ethiopia. They decided to raise money to help with this crisis in the best way they knew – through music. The pair wrote a song, 'Do They Know It's Christmas?', and persuaded leading British and Irish singers to record it. None of the performers – recording under the name Band Aid – received a fee, and the record went straight to number one in the charts, where it stayed for five weeks.

Geldof had hoped to raise £70,000 for famine relief, but the Band Aid song raised millions. A similar song, 'We Are the World', was recorded by mainly American musicians in early 1985. It, too, raised millions for famine relief. The success of the two songs, and the musicians' eagerness to take part, led Geldof to organize a massive live concert in mid-1985. On 13 July, concerts in two venues (Wembley Stadium in London and JFK Stadium in Philadelphia) staged the Live Aid event. The concert was one of the most-watched events ever to appear on television, with about 400 million viewers watching in more than 60 countries.

Throughout Live Aid, viewers were urged to pledge money for famine relief. Like the Band Aid recording, it far exceeded the organizers' hopes in raising money. Having set a target of £1 million, the Live Aid organizers received more than £150 million. In addition, the event showed that large amounts of money could be raised quickly through skilful use of the media. Since 1985, dozens of similar fund-raising appeals (often using the name Aid in their titles) have raised millions for charitable causes.

Voluntary groups (which are less often known by the old-fashioned term charities) raise money from individuals and businesses. They don't take money from governments or international organizations and because of that they need not take orders from those sources. Such groups are called non-governmental organizations (NGOs) to reflect their independence.

NGOs often work alongside aid teams representing donor countries or international organizations. In fact, not being linked to any specific developed country can make it easier for NGOs such as Oxfam, Save the Children or Christian Aid to forge links in countries that need aid.

Governments sometimes offer special tax deals to voluntary groups. The UK system of gift aid allows charity to reclaim the tax donors have paid on the money they give to charity. If a UK taxpayer donates £100 to Oxfam, the charity can claim back the tax he paid on that £100 under gift aid, making his £100 donation worth nearer to £125.

Performers gather on stage at the end of the Live Aid concert in July 1985. The event raised more than £150 million and paved the way for similar international fund-raising events in the following decades.

Putting money to work

No one likes to see money wasted,
especially money that should be spent on improving the lives of the poorest people in the world. When millions are being spent on a project – and billions overall – the people who deliver international aid must prove that they are spending the money well.

In January 2008, the Wall Street Journal newspaper published details from a review the World Bank was conducting on how its money was being spent. The review concentrated on five health projects in India, totalling $569 million (£345 million) in loans. Some of the information pointed to massive inefficiency and waste.

The World Bank review found that corruption took 90 per cent of the budget of one project. A major project to control HIV/AIDS, worth $194 million (£118 million), used faulty test kits which could produce the wrong results – causing the disease to spread even more quickly. An $82 million (£49 million) health project in Orissa, one of India's poorest states, was doing little to improve the dirty, badly equipped hospitals that World Bank observers visited.

Some people might look at this evidence – and the massive amounts of money at stake – and conclude that aid itself is a bad idea. They could argue that humans are fallible and that given a chance, people will pocket money that is meant for needier people. Supporters of aid projects need to point to some positive results to ensure that aid continues to flow to those who need it.

African success story

Not all aid projects are badly managed and wasteful. A bilateral aid project in East Africa has combined effectiveness and value for money, while also halting the advance of a desert and restoring good farmland. The Wei Wei Integrated Development Project (WWIDP) was begun in 1987 as a partnership between the governments of Kenya and Italy.

The project is an irrigation scheme about 500 km north of the Kenyan capital, Nairobi. The fast-flowing Wei Wei River runs northwards through foothills in the region, above a wide expanse of plains. For many years, the local Pokot people have struggled to earn a living farming those plains. The soil has the potential to support a wide range of crops, but rainfall is irregular and droughts are common.

The WWIDP has two main aims – to irrigate the plains by diverting some water from the Wei Wei River, and to help local Pokot families develop productive farming techniques. About £4.5 million of Italian money helped to fund a gravity-powered irrigation system running

Opposite: a vast mound of grain and other food lies rotting at an aid depot in North Lokichokio, northern Kenya. The food was sent for homeless people in Darfur, a war-torn region in neighbouring Sudan, but it was impossible to distribute the food because of fighting.

Accountability

No matter how an aid project develops – through multilateral channels, government-to-government efforts or from money donated by ordinary people – it must use funds and equipment in the best way possible.

It is easy to waste money through inefficiency or corruption, which is why it is important to keep a close eye on such projects. No one likes to see money wasted, especially money intended to improve the health and living conditions of the world's neediest people.

Aid agencies use many terms to describe how they monitor projects – and how the wider world can monitor the agencies themselves. One such term is transparency, which means that information on how money is spent must be clear and available to the public. Taxpayers and people donating to charities want their aid money to go to projects rather than being spent on employing lawyers and accountants, or to furnish expensive offices in big cities.

A related term is accountability, which comes from the word accountable. Like transparency, accountability is a both a goal and a requirement of aid projects and aid organizations themselves. Members at every level of these organizations must be able to explain what they do and to account for the money they spend. This responsibility should extend right down to field workers who buy the petrol for project vehicles, the food for the staff and pay the mobile phone bills connected to a project.

Individual projects, departments of multilateral organizations and the organizations themselves can be threatened by poor accountability. The British public was shocked, in mid-2009, to learn how many MPs had claimed government money for new houses, furniture and even dog food. The international community becomes just as angry when it learns about bad management and greed among people involved with aid.

down into the plain. Another £2 million helped to set up 540 individual farm plots for families. The final phase has been to provide business and marketing advice so that the Pokot farmers can sell their crops most effectively.

The scheme now helps farmers produce crops worth more than £4 million every year in the irrigated region. The project is sustainable because the irrigation relies on a simple force – gravity – combined with a steady supply of water. As a result, the project was recognized as a success story by the United Nations Environment Programme.

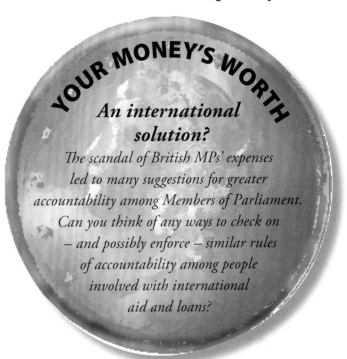

YOUR MONEY'S WORTH

An international solution?

The scandal of British MPs' expenses led to many suggestions for greater accountability among Members of Parliament. Can you think of any ways to check on – and possibly enforce – similar rules of accountability among people involved with international aid and loans?

A Christian woman is given medicine for her child at a relief camp in the state of Orissa in eastern India in 2008. Clashes between Hindus and Christians left many people homeless and afraid to leave their villages.

Stacking the cards

Some people in developed countries

question how wisely international aid and loan money is spent, but many of the poorer nations criticize the system behind international aid. They argue that it automatically favours richer countries – and the economic values that they hold – while allowing poorer countries little chance to influence how money is distributed.

Theory and practice

As well as the issue of who controls aid, another big issue is how people decide which projects deserve funding. Even more tricky is the question of which governments deserve support (through international aid) and which may either be corrupt or have failed in other ways.

Organizations and countries who provide aid do need to exercise some control over it. People who ask a bank for a mortgage or a loan for a car, for example, must prove that they will spend the money on either a house or a car. But the world of international aid is more complicated, even though a great deal of aid comes in the form of loans.

The developed countries which provide much of the money for international organizations, such as the World Bank and IMF, often project their own values when thinking about aid. For example, during the 1980s the governments of the US, the UK and several other developed countries believed strongly in spending cuts and low taxes for their own citizens. They wanted the countries which received international aid to adopt similar policies. Many of those countries would not – and, they added, could not – follow that example.

As a result, some countries found they received less aid or had extra conditions imposed on the aid they did receive.

This sort of 'rich versus poor' conflict breeds resentment, and international leaders now try to find more points of agreement. But the issue remains important, especially if some developing countries believe that extra conditions on their aid lock them into a state of constant poverty.

YOUR MONEY'S WORTH

Considering conditions

One of the biggest criticisms of the IMF and the World Bank centres on the conditions a country must agree to in order to receive loans or aid. Many people argue that by imposing such restrictions these powerful organizations are interfering in the way that countries govern themselves. In other words, they force developing countries to adopt policies that might work for richer countries, but may not work for them. Their defenders, however, say that the conditions are necessary to ensure that the money is used wisely and leads to real progress. Can you think of any conditions that you would consider unreasonable or essential?

Many developing countries have unfair political systems, which make it difficult for aid to reach people. Zimbabwean police threaten a supporter of the opposition leader Morgan Tsvangirai.

The debt burden

Paying back a loan can become difficult
for an individual, a family… or even a country.
Unexpected events can cause problems. For example,
a father might lose his job and ask his bank for
a payment holiday to help the family's finances
while he looks for another job. Similarly, a country
can find it difficult to meet loan repayments if it
has suffered a crisis such as a poor harvest, severe
drought, warfare or other disasters.

The governments of those countries face a difficult choice: they can either struggle to meet the terms of the loans (and risk creating greater hardship in their countries) or withhold the repayments which may mean that the amount they owe increases rapidly.

Opposite: young protesters march through the rain near the headquarters of the IMF and World Bank in Washington, DC. Like many young people around the world, they are calling for an end to the international debt burden in the developing world.

Many developing countries borrowed large amounts of money from the World Bank, the IMF, banks in developed (richer) countries and the governments of the developed countries. Some of the borrowing countries were ruled by dictators or corrupt governments, so the borrowed money fell into the wrong hands.

Others spent the loan money on projects, but have since had to cope with natural or man-made disasters. Either way, the citizens of many developing countries now suffer because of the financial penalties tied in with the loans. The problems can be enough to condemn some countries to remain constantly in poverty for as long as the loan is outstanding.

Campaigning efforts

Many anti-poverty campaigners around the world have concentrated on removing this debt burden from the poorest countries. Since 2000, their efforts have been rewarded – a number of multilateral lending organizations, as well as national governments, have reduced the amount of debt owed to them. Some of the debt, though, has only been rescheduled rather than being wiped out. The borrowing countries still have to repay the money.

Anti-debt groups point out that a decade into the new century – and several years into the worldwide credit crunch – Third World debt remains a huge concern. The Jubilee Debt Campaign points out that the poorest countries have to pay almost £66 million every day to richer countries. Overall, the poorest 49 countries owe a total of £250 billion. The debt of the poorest 144 countries (most of the world apart

Personal account

GOING BACK IN TIME?

Bono, the lead singer of the Irish rock group U2, is as well known for supporting aid for the developing world as he is for his music. During an interview in 2004 about this work, Bono was asked whether cancelling Africa's massive debt was an act of charity or of justice. His response looked back to harsher times in the nineteenth century: 'You know, in the nineteenth century, they used to put people in prison for bad debts. It was barbaric and it was very inefficient. The family could not make any money and pay back the debts, or whatever. We've stopped doing that now to people, but we're still doing it to countries – holding these poorest of the poor to ransom for debts of their grandparents.'

from western Europe, North America, Japan, Australia and New Zealand) is a staggering $2.9 trillion (£1.8 trillion).

Ultimately, it is up to the richer, developed countries to change existing debt arrangements. They have a much larger stake in funding international aid and lending organizations (such as the IMF and World Bank), which gives them greater influence within those bodies.

The leaders of the richest nations meet regularly and exchange ideas: debt relief

Bono shares his views on international aid with US president George W. Bush at an informal meeting in the White House in 2005.

YOUR MONEY'S WORTH

Dropping the debt

Not everyone agrees with the idea of dropping the debt burden that developing countries have accumulated. It could be argued that simply walking away from an agreement as important as a national loan sets a bad example for the people in a country – and could damage that country's financial institutions. Do you think this is a convincing argument?

has been a topic since the 1990s. Discussions eventually led to the formation of a group called the Heavily Indebted Poor Countries (HIPC) in 1996. The 37 countries in this group can gain debt relief from the World Bank and IMF in return for accepting some strict conditions.

In January 2005 Gordon Brown (who was then UK chancellor) called for the world's richest countries to cancel developing world debt by the end of that year. That suggestion gained support; after a meeting of the G8 in July 2005 the debt relief became debt cancellation. The Multilateral Debt Relief Initiative (MDRI) scheme carried the process further. It offered the cancellation of all multilateral debts owed by HIPC countries to the IMF, the World Bank and the African Development Bank.

Campaigners welcome these changes but they note – as the statistics at the start of this chapter point out – that many poor countries are not part of the HIPC and that many debts are owed to other lenders.

Different voices

A number of people, representing very different points of view, are calling for widespread changes in the way international aid and loans operate. Some believe that the system is too open to bribery and inefficiency to do any good. Others believe it is a necessary tool to help people and nations move forward, provided those people and nations have a say in how the money is distributed and spent.

Then there are those who believe that aid is a bad thing in itself because countries come to depend on hand-outs rather than building a future on their own.

Even though these opinions are so varied, they provide a chance to re-examine the aid system and move forward with one that is both efficient and generous. In fact, the credit crunch and the international economic crisis have led many organizations to re-examine their entire structure in order to see how they can adapt to troubled times. Private companies, government departments, charities and even individuals are looking inward to see how best they can face the outside world. Those involved with international aid are in good company.

More equal than others

Countries which receive aid for bilateral projects cannot expect much control over the amount of money provided and how it is spent. The bilateral arrangement is clear: one country has money to spend, and its voters believe they have the right to know where their tax money is going. At its most extreme, this opinion is equivalent to saying: 'we are being kind enough to provide you with this money, so just be grateful'.

Multilateral projects are more complicated, although voting also lies at the heart of some people's views. The World Bank and the IMF are both made up of many member states, but decisions on how and where to spend money are not always decided by a simple majority. The president of the World Bank, for example, has always been American. Also, the richest countries (which provide the most money) have more voting power over IMF decisions than other member states which might be receiving IMF money.

A 'going out of business' sign on a US store in 2009 highlights the difficulties faced by all countries – not just those traditionally considered the poorest – during the credit crunch.

Personal account

CHANGE FROM THE GROUND UP

Some NGOs are changing the whole aid process to link donors and projects more closely, while giving a greater voice to local people at grass roots level. GlobalGiving is one such organization. Potential donors can log on to its website and choose from dozens of aid projects around the world, ranging from rainforest preservation in Brazil to using sport to help young people with disabilities in Kenya. All the funds are monitored, so that donors can be confident that their money will not be wasted through inefficiency and corruption.

The projects are usually organized and run by local people, rather than foreigners who have recently arrived and are unfamiliar with a country and its customs. The organizers provide field reports, which can be read online to give a flavour of how the money is spent. Doctor Chukwumuanya Igboekwu is part of an organization called Physicians for Social Justice (PSJ). GlobalGiving has helped to fund the Preventing Childhood Malaria Death Project in rural Nigeria.

In one of his field reports, Doctor Igboekwu writes about the project's success at a local level: 'At Manigi village, the project team encountered a mother who had trekked about 10 kilometers on foot from a neighbouring village to present her nine-month-old baby for treatment. She heard the news about the visit of our malaria team who will be offering free malaria treatment to children from one of her friends. The mobile team treated her sick child and provided her with an insecticide treated net. She was full of gratitude to our sponsors and all those who provided the resources that made it possible for her baby to get both free malaria treatment and a treated bed net.'

The influence of developed countries over developing countries has been a source of resentment for many years. The simmering tensions have had serious consequences for some of the world's neediest people, as different governments argue over who deserves international aid, and on what terms. The same arguments are played out in the UK, the United States and in other developed countries where the main political parties have opposing views on the value of international aid.

American radio talk show presenters often express extreme views on political subjects. Rush Limbaugh, shown here, often argues against sending money to other countries as loans or aid.

The main debates about international aid take place in all sorts of news sources – in newspapers and magazines, on the Internet and on television. But some of the fiercest arguments rage on talk radio stations in the United States and in some other countries. Presenters become nationally famous for stirring up opposing opinions – often insulting those who disagree with them as tempers flare.

YOUR MONEY'S WORTH

Why not?

Why shouldn't the world's richest countries have more voting power in the big international economic organizations? After all, they're the ones who are paying for all this! Do you agree or disagree with that statement? In either case, how would you argue the point with someone who took the opposite view?

New generations

Children and younger people are at the heart of international aid. They are often at the receiving end of medical and educational aid projects. Governments and aid agencies alike target children in their strategies for development: it is vital that a country's young can develop and grow without fear of disease, ignorance or harsh working conditions.

Opposite: children from different backgrounds study together at a school in North Carolina, USA. They will be part of the next generation aiming to reduce inequalities around the world.

These young people will become the adults of the future, with some of them taking their places in government departments, aid agencies and even in the international organizations that will determine the future of international aid for future generations.

In the picture

The inner workings of IMF loans or government aid budgets are often too complicated for people – young or old – to understand and digest. Luckily, there are ways to learn more about the subject and even begin to play a part. The World Bank's youth website, known as youthink!, is an excellent introduction to the world of international aid and how the bank operates. It is neither oversimplified nor dull – multimedia sections, blogs, photo galleries and 'webitorials' present a wide range of opinions on the subject.

Most young people learn about international development and aid through NGOs such as Oxfam, Save the Children or the International Red Cross. Like the World Bank, these organizations welcome involvement from young people. Fund-raising projects enable young people to come to grips with some of the trickier issues surrounding aid – simply because they need to know how to explain them to others.

Particular campaigns, rather than specific organizations, have inspired many young people to do more. In June 2005, pop star turned anti-poverty campaigner Bob Geldof addressed 100,000 festival-goers from Glastonbury's Pyramid Stage. 'I want you to individually believe that you can change the condition of the most put-upon and beaten-down people on this planet', he told the crowd before urging them to link hands and say 'Make poverty history.' Perhaps in 20 or 30 years' time a middle-aged government official will remember her teenage festival experience and push for even greater change.

Raising awareness – and survival rates

Sometimes organizations that aim to help children can work with the children themselves to achieve progress, especially in areas that adults feel are overwhelming. The widespread and deadly disease HIV/AIDS is one such area. Everyone agrees it is devastating, but many adults are overwhelmed by the scale of the problem and the speed with which the virus has spread across the globe.

Children – and people who spend time with them – are less likely to ignore a problem such as HIV/AIDS simply because it is so widespread. The UN agency Unicef has found some messages of hope amid the gloom surrounding this disease and it has put together a plan to fight its spread.

At the heart of the campaign are some of the facts that stop some people in their tracks. Every day, about 1000 children become infected with the HIV virus. Most of those children contract the virus before they are born, at delivery or while breastfeeding. Without treatment, a third of those infected babies will die before their first birthday, and half before their second birthday.

A common reaction to such statistics is for people to shake their heads and say 'isn't it awful' and 'we really should do something about that'… and then quietly ignore the issue. Unicef has introduced awareness-raising campaigns with a focus on children and an international reach. Unite for Children, Unite against AIDS, for example, mobilizes support (including donations) to educate people about the disease.

On a local level, Unicef has helped to fund and operate programmes which provide essential medicines for children who have been infected. In the West African country of Niger, Unicef contributes to more than 150 health centres. These are often the only places where people can meet medical professionals. Pregnant women can be treated for the virus and babies and toddlers can receive medicines to help them battle the disease in their crucial first two years.

Unicef has also helped mothers who have lost their husbands to find work and even create their own businesses by providing loans that can be repaid over many years.

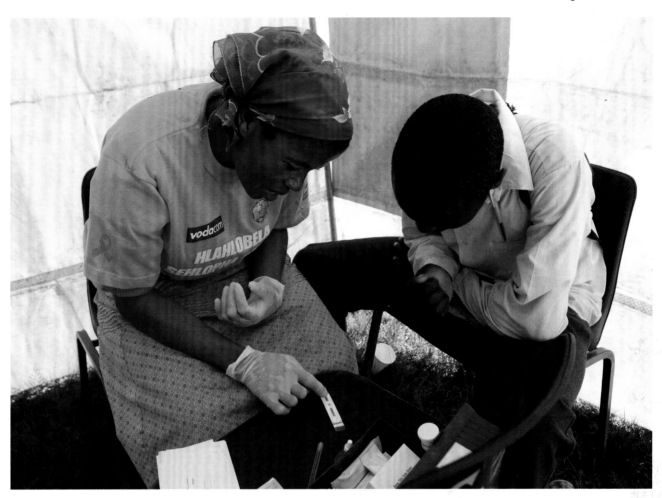

THE GIFT OF LIFE

M. Adama Ouedraogo is a Unicef Niger health specialist and spells out the core strategy of the nationwide battle to provide children with medical weapons to combat HIV/AIDS: 'It is important that HIV-infected children do not miss out on the medical treatment they need… that is specific to their age and their condition.'

Sixteen-year-old Mikiea Rakuba is tested at an HIV/AIDS awareness event for schoolchildren in the southern African country of Lesotho. The event was organized in 2007 by Unicef and the NGO Kick4Life.

Focus on the future

International aid and loans are an important element of the world economy. Since that economy hit troubled times in 2007, a question mark hangs over the future of aid, loans and development generally. Political leaders in even the richest countries are trying to find ways to reduce spending – especially when so many people within their own borders are losing their jobs or finding times tough.

Reports published in early 2009 painted a bleak picture for some of the world's poorest countries, especially those in Africa. The world

Enlightened self-interest

Imagine being able to help someone else and in the process gaining some benefit. That happy combination is called enlightened self-interest, and national leaders try to achieve it with their actions and long-term policies. In May 2009, US president Barack Obama announced his aim to spend $63 billion (£41 billion) over the following six years to combat disease and improve children's health in many of the world's poorest countries.

This plan follows on from a similar strategy that the previous president, George W. Bush, used to provide medical aid to developing countries. Both men – like other national leaders – recognized that such actions help to build friendship while at the same time improving living conditions in the poorer countries.

Jack Lew, a senior member of the Obama government, stressed this link between wide-ranging aid and diplomacy: 'When we talk about development and diplomacy, we mean the United States needs to be affirmatively active in dealing with some of the root causes of instability in so many poor countries. If people can't provide for the basic needs of their family... it's a dangerous situation.'

Opposite: containers await shipment at the upgraded port at Jakarta, the capital of Indonesia. Some developing countries, such as Indonesia, are breaking free of their dependence on international aid and becoming important trading nations in their own right.

price for commodities such as coffee and grains – important export earners for Africa – had fallen by 20 per cent in the previous two years. Countries such as Bangladesh, which export clothing to Europe and North America, have seen their incomes drop as people have less money to spend on those goods.

Just as worrying is the fact that the amount of aid flowing to these poorer countries looks likely to fall. Developed countries have promised to devote a percentage of their GDP to international aid (see pages 12-15) but with the economies of those richer countries shrinking, that aid total also shrinks.

Glossary

African Development Bank   An international bank which provides aid and loans to help development in Africa.

aid   Money given to a country to help its development.

bilateral   Involving two parties, eg the donor and recipient country in a bilateral aid project.

chancellor   The British government member responsible for national economic policy.

cold war   A period lasting roughly from 1945 to 1991 during which the United States and the Soviet Union opposed each other and nearly went to war several times.

commodity   A natural product that can be traded on its own (such as tea) or as a raw material (such as copper or iron).

Commonwealth   A group of 53 independent nations, most of which were once ruled by Great Britain.

communist   A political system in which all property is owned by the community and each person contributes and receives according to ability and needs. The government provides work, health care, education and housing, but may deny people certain freedoms.

corruption   Dishonesty in government or business, especially involving money.

credit   A banking term to describe lending and how easy it is to arrange it.

credit crunch   A period beginning in 2007 during which credit and other economic measures were severely affected.

debt relief   A reduction in a loan repayment, or a cancellation of a debt.

developed countries   Countries with a long history of industrial production, usually among the wealthiest in the world.

developing countries   Countries with little or no history of industrial production, often among the poorest in the world.

donor   An individual, organization or country that gives (donates) something.

export   To sell abroad, or what is sold abroad.

fallible   Not perfect; likely to make mistakes or to be misled.

grant   Money that is given and which does not need to be repaid.

gross domestic product   The total goods and services produced by a country.

loan   An amount of money borrowed from a bank which must be repaid in full over an agreed period.

malaria   A potentially deadly disease spread by mosquitoes.

multilateral   Involving three or more groups.

non-governmental organization   An international organization composed of volunteers rather than elected government members.

propaganda   Information (not always true) that is spread to change people's minds about an issue.

raw material   A basic ingredient (such as wood) used to make something else.

recipient   An individual, organization or country that receives something.

reschedule (of a debt)   To provide easier terms for repayment.

Second World War   The war beginning in Europe but spreading around the world between 1939 and 1945.

self-interest   Protecting one's own interests.

simple majority   An election in which the group with more than half the votes wins.

Soviet Union   The name given to a country that included Russia and 14 of its neighbours, which united to form a larger communist country from 1917 to 1991.

sustainable   Able to be repeated many times.

tax   Money that individuals and companies must pay to their national government, which pays for services such as health care and education.

transparency   Having all dealings open for examination by anyone.

United Nations   An international organization made up of 192 independent countries which aims to promote worldwide peace and cooperation.

western   Developed countries that do not have communist governments.

Further reading

Aid to Africa Debra A. Miller (ed) (Greenhaven, 2009)

Rich World, Poor World Melanie Jarman (Franklin Watts, 2006)

The World Bank and the International Monetary Fund Peggy Kahn (ed) (Chelsea House, 2009)

Websites

ActionAid International
http://www.actionaid.org/index.aspx

Jubilee Debt Campaign
http://www.jubileedebtcampaign.org.uk

GlobalGiving
http://www.globalgiving.co.uk

youthink!
http://youthink.worldbank.org/

Index